A ROOKIE BIOGRAPHY

MARGARETE STEIFF

Toy Maker

By Carol Greene

CHILDRENS PRESS®
CHICAGO

This book is for Bianca Baker.

Margarete Steiff (1847-1909)

Library of Congress Cataloging-in-Publication Data

Greene, Carol.
    Margarete Steiff : toy maker / by Carol Greene.
      p.   cm. — (A Rookie biography)
    Includes index.
    Summary: A biography of the German toy maker, stricken during
childhood by polio, whose company became famous for its teddy bears.
    ISBN 0-516-04257-2
    1. Steiff, Margarete, 1847-1909—Juvenile literature. 2. Teddy bear
makers—German—Biography—Juvenile literature. [1. Steiff, Margarete,
1847-1909. 2. Toymakers. 3. Physically handicapped.] I. Title. II. Series:
Greene, Carol. Rookie biography.
NK8740.5.S74G74   1993
688.7′2′092—dc20
[B]   93-16855
                                            CIP
                                            AC

Margarete Steiff
was a real person.
(*Steiff* rhymes with *life*.)
She lived from 1847 to 1909.
Margarete could not walk.
But she built
one of the world's
best toy companies.
This is her story.

TABLE OF CONTENTS

Traditional German architecture of the 1800s

Chapter 1

The Girl in a Cart

The little German town
of Giengen slept
in the afternoon sun.
Birds sang quiet songs
and the River Brenz
flowed gently by.

Then the church clock chimed.
School was out!
Down the street came
clatters and shouts.
It was Margarete Steiff
and her friends.

Margarete had polio
when she was 18 months old.
Now she could not walk.
So each day her sisters
and neighbor children
pulled her to and from school
in a small wooden cart.

Margarete liked school.
She learned fast.
She liked to play too.
She sat in her cart
and made up games to play
with the other children.

But sometimes her friends
got excited and ran away.
They forgot that Margarete
could not run with them.

Then Margarete would call
the little children to her side
and play with them.
She always liked little children.

At home, Margarete played
with her big sisters,
Pauline and Marie, and
her little brother, Fritz.
Sometimes she slid
along the floor
to keep up with them.

Then Margarete was in trouble.

"You are ruining your clothes,"
her mother would scold.
"No more sliding!"

Mrs. Steiff was strict
with all her children.
She didn't baby Margarete
because she couldn't walk.

Later, Margarete said
she was glad about that.
Her mother helped her
become a strong person.

Margarete's parents
worried about her, though.
They took her to many doctors.
But doctors in those days
knew very little about polio.
They couldn't help Margarete.

"Who will take care of
Margarete after we die?"
worried her parents.
But Margarete didn't worry.
She believed that God
would take care of her.

She rode in her cart.
She studied and played.
And sometimes she got into trouble.
Margarete was happy.

Chapter 2

Some Little Elephants

"May I go to sewing school?"
Margarete asked her parents.

They didn't know if
Margarete could sew.
The polio had left
her arms and hands weak.
But they said yes anyway.

At first, Margarete made many
mistakes in her sewing.
And her right arm often hurt.
She kept trying, though,
and she got better and better.

Margarete's brother, Fritz,
was her best friend.
When he went away to
school in another town,
she felt a little sad.

"May I take zither lessons?"
Margarete asked her parents.

The zither is a flat musical
instrument with strings.
Her parents didn't know if
Margarete could play it at all.
But they said yes anyway.

And Margarete *could* play.
Soon she played so well
that she gave lessons to others.

Margarete made money
with those lessons.
She used the money to buy
a sewing machine
—the first one in town.
Then she made money sewing.

Margarete sewed felt clothes
for adults and children.
(Felt is a heavy, warm fabric.)
She was always careful.
Each thing she made
had to be just right.

"Why don't you open a shop?"
said a friend one day.

So Margarete did,
right in her parents' home.
Soon Margarete's shop
was so busy that
she had to hire helpers.

Then one day, Margarete
was looking at a magazine.
In it she saw a pattern
for a little elephant.

"I could make that,"
thought Margarete.
"I could make it of felt
and stuff it with wool."

So Margarete made
some little elephants.
She gave them
to grown-ups as pincushions
and to children as toys.
Everyone loved them.

A Steiff elephant made of felt. An elephant
was Margarete's first toy animal.

One winter day, Margarete
sold eight little elephants.
She didn't know it then,
but that was the start
of a new life for her.

Chapter 3

The Toy Factory

Years went by and
Fritz Steiff grew up.
He got married
and had nine children.

Fritz thought Margarete's
elephants were wonderful.

"Give me a sack of them
to take to the fair," he said.

Margarete did and
Fritz sold every one.

The German city of Stuttgart as it looks today

Then he took more elephants
to the big city of Stuttgart.
He sold them too.

Soon Margarete's shop
turned into a toy factory.
She and Fritz worked together
and the children ran in and out.

Fritz learned how to
make the elephants stronger.
Then Margarete made a donkey
that the children could ride.

"We need more room!"
Fritz kept saying.
At last Margarete agreed.
So the Margarete Steiff
Felt Toy Factory
moved to a big new house.

A sampling of Steiff stuffed toys, including lions, rabbits, dogs, and monkeys

Soon they were making
other toy animals—
cats and dogs,
camels and pigs,
monkeys and mice,
and rabbits.

They hired people to work
in the factory and
people to work at home.

Many of the workers were women.
Margarete looked after them.
Each must have enough work.
But no one must have too much.
And each toy must be perfect.

Margarete let the women
keep their babies at work—
safe in a crib beside them.
If a worker was sick
or in trouble, Margarete
found a way to help.

Those workers became part
of Margarete's family.

Musician dolls play in a Steiff toy band.

As time passed,
the toy factory kept growing.
They began to make dolls.
They sold toys in other countries.
Even princes and princesses
played with Margarete's toys.

But the best toy of all
was yet to come.

Some of the first bears made by the Steiff toy factory

Chapter 4

Bears!

More years passed and
Margarete's nephews grew up.
One by one, they came
to work in the toy factory.

Richard was first.
He had studied art
and was full of ideas.

Richard knew the factory
already made toy bears.
But they weren't soft and cuddly.
Richard wanted to make a bear
that was more like a doll.
So he looked at pictures of
bears he had drawn in school.

Margarete Steiff (left),
and Richard Steiff with
a Steiff teddy bear (below).

Then Richard made a pattern
and showed it to Margarete.
She found some soft gray plush
and made the bear.
He was a cute little fellow.
But at first no one wanted him.

Then Richard took some bears
to a toy fair in Leipzig.
An American toy-seller saw them.

"I'll take 3,000!" he said.

The fair in Leipzig (above), where Richard Steiff sold
3,000 bears, and the square as it looks today (below).

The World's Fair in St. Louis, Missouri, was held in 1904.

This is one of the oldest teddy bears in the world.
It is kept in the Steiff collection in Germany.

Next, Margarete sent
her nephew Franz
to the World's Fair
in St. Louis, Missouri.
He took some bears along and soon
his book was full of orders.

Before long,
everyone wanted
a toy bear—
men, women,
and, of course,
children. Other
companies began
to make bears too.

Children all over the
world loved teddy bears.

BUTTON IN EAR

"We must find a way
to make our bears special,"
said Margarete.
"People must know that
they have a Steiff bear."

"Let's put a metal button in
each bear's ear," said Franz.
So they did.

Now they needed more room again.
Richard drew up plans for
a factory with glass walls.
That gave the workers more light.

And more people wanted the bears.
They called them "Teddy bears" now,
after Theodore (Teddy) Roosevelt,
president of the United States.

The teddy bear was
named for President
Theodore (Teddy) Roosevelt.

And Margarete's
workers kept
turning out bears—
one beautiful bear
after another.

Steiff bears come in
many sizes and colors.
Some even run for president.

Margarete Steiff in her office at the toy factory (below)

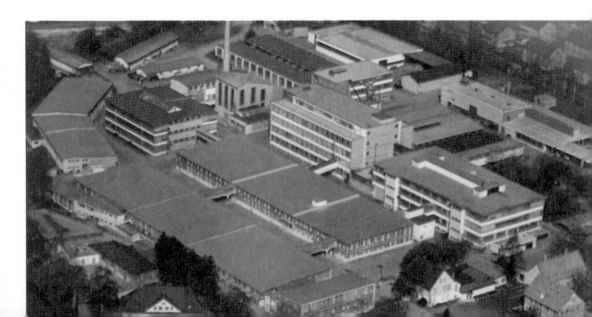

Chapter 5

"Only the Best"

Margarete Steiff was
a happy woman.

Her parents had worried
about who would take care of her.
But here she was—
taking care of her whole family
and thousands of workers too.

She had no children of her own.
But the children of
Giengen loved her.
They called her "Auntie Margarete"
and asked her to
tell them stories.

And she made children happy
all over the world
with her lovable, cuddly toys.

"Only the best is
good enough for children,"
she always told her workers.

Stuffed lions and leopards

Margarete believed that.
She made sure that
each new toy felt
just right to a child.

Margarete Steiff died
on May 9, 1909.
She was 61 years old.

People at the toy factory
said they felt as if
they had lost their heart.
How could they go on?

But Margarete's family
has gone on with her work,
making dolls and toys
and teddy bears—
"only the best" for children.

Opposite page: Margarete Steiff with one of her teddy bears. Above: Steiff bears are known by the button in the ear. Below left: Steiff Christmas dolls and stuffed animals. Below right: An alligator hand puppet.

Important Dates

1847   July 24—Born in Giengen, Württemberg, Germany, to Maria Margarete and Friedrich Steiff

1877   Opened shop in parents' home

1880   Made and sold first felt elephants

1889   Moved toy factory to new building in Muehlstrasse

1893   Registered company as official business

1894   Made first Steiff dolls

1897   Richard Steiff began working for the company

1903   First teddy bear designed and made
First glass building for new factory completed

1904   Showed toys at World's Fair, St. Louis, Missouri; won Grand Prize

1909   May 9—Died in Giengen

INDEX

Page numbers in boldface type indicate illustrations.

PHOTO CREDITS

ABOUT THE AUTHOR

Carol Greene has degrees in English literature and musicology. She has worked in international exchange programs, as an editor, and as a teacher of writing. She now lives in Webster Groves, Missouri, and writes full-time. She has published more than 100 books, including those in the Childrens Press Rookie Biographies series.